Unfolding

Poems Along the Arc of Becoming

Erika Haynes

India | USA | UK

Copyright © Erika Haynes
All Rights Reserved.

This book has been self-published with all reasonable efforts taken to make the material error-free by the author. No part of this book shall be used, reproduced in any manner whatsoever without written permission from the author, except in the case of brief quotations embodied in critical articles and reviews.

The Author of this book is solely responsible and liable for its content including but not limited to the views, representations, descriptions, statements, information, opinions, and references ["Content"]. The Content of this book shall not constitute or be construed or deemed to reflect the opinion or expression of the Publisher or Editor. Neither the Publisher nor Editor endorse or approve the Content of this book or guarantee the reliability, accuracy, or completeness of the Content published herein and do not make any representations or warranties of any kind, express or implied, including but not limited to the implied warranties of merchantability, fitness for a particular purpose.

The Publisher and Editor shall not be liable whatsoever...

Made with ❤ on the BookLeaf Publishing Platform
www.bookleafpub.in
www.bookleafpub.com

Dedication

To the beautiful women I have laughed, cried, and
evolved with—thank you.
You are each a part of my soul.

Preface

Along life's journey, our soul grows with us and guides that growth.
We experience emotions so profound they shape us; each moment molds the next.
A soul's path is never straight—it bends, circles, ascends —each turn a lesson, each season a threshold.
These poems gather those moments, mapping the arc of one soul's becoming.

Acknowledgements

I acknowledge the shaping of my soul through the host
of the Universe
and every form of its energy and truth.

I honor the ancestors—mine and others—
who handed down fragments of their own journeys
so we might continue the path.

I recognize the work each of us invests
in this unfolding,
and I light a candle
so that we do not forget.

1. Invocation

Before words,
there was breath—
the quiet promise
of beginning.

Before angst,
there was pulse,
the steady rhythm
beneath the ache of becoming.

I was always here,
waiting beneath the noise,
listening for myself to return.

Now,
I begin again—
not new,
but known.

2. It's Simple

It's simple—draw an "M,"
connect the bottom.
Glass shoes. Tulle dreams.
Happily ever after.
Six years old.

"That's love," they said.
He pulled my hair—
teasing, tugging, endless jokes.
Happily ever after.
Nine years old.

"It's simple," he reminded me.
Slid his hand—
searching, stealing, violating.
Fifteen years old.

"It's simple," he sneered.
Hits. Punches. Slaps.
Obey.

Twenty-one years old.

Kissing, hugging, playing,
lifting my daughter in the air.
"It's simple," he said,
cocked the gun.
Thirty didn't seem great.

Crying. Reeling. Widow.
Among the living, unseen.
"It's simple," on the wind.
Thirty-nine years old.

"It's simple," he said—
brought me coffee, flowers,
dug through granite,
unearthed my heart.
Forty-three years old.

It's holding, not owning.
Speaking, not saving.
Happily human.
Never simple.
Fifty years old.

3. Wrinkles

Her wrinkles tell her story—
    the life she lived,
      her victories,
        her hardships.

    I knew her before
    the wrinkles of time.

I remember when life gave her
        each one.

    Every line, every frown,
    each angry moment,
      and the laughter
        in between.

    My brother carved
    the ones of worry—
    sneaking out at night,
    laughter in taillights.

My father etched
the lines of pain.
Divorce
leaves its mark.

Her friends softened
her with smile lines—
sunburned shoulders,
salt in her hair.

And I,
I caused the most,
because
I
refused.

4. The Wrong Ways

You took me with you
in all the wrong ways—
carried pieces of me
the wrong way round.

You walked away,
and silence filled the floor.
I rose,　　　but only halfway.

Fooled you.

I cry
behind the door;
smiles lie on the other side.

The pain
folds me in half.

I vomit
my love

5. My Voice

You sneered and broke my heart today,
while standing in the rain.
You looked right through my trembling face—
you never saw my pain.

I tried to speak my mind today,
after all these years,
to loose what's long been bottled up,
and stumbled through my tears.

That smile you wear - it holds me still,
demands I play my role.
No one cares to hear me speak—
a gut punch to my soul.

Happy talk and rhyming lines,
to lift the room's gray mood.
I bite my lip and hold it in,
and try not to be rude.

6. I Choose Me

The alarm cracks the shell of sleep,
shaking something deep inside
until my eyes flutter open.

Thoughts rush in—
I freeze,
pause.

Today, I choose me.

Water carries me forward,
steam blurs the edges of thought.

In the mirror, I question
hair, face, the familiar stranger.

I breathe in,
release.

Today, I choose me.

Meeting after meeting—
my pen fills the page:
to do, to learn, to vanish in the noise.

I stare at the first bullet,
anchor myself,
begin.

Today, I choose me.

I claim my space in the chair—
goddess, builder, maker of calm.
Nurturer. Collaborator. Flame.

I straighten,
adjust.

Today, I choose me.

Evening settles. Slippers on,
book in hand,
the air thick with asks.

Can you?
I need.
Please.

I raise my hand,
and everything stills.

Today, I choose me.

7. The Clearing

Salt water at the broom's edge,
sage smoke curls through rooms,
soft as forgiveness.

I sweep what lingers—
dust, doubt, the stale breath of yesterday.
Each stroke a small forgetting,
each spark a prayer.

A candle flickers in the corner,
its flame unsure but holding.
Shadows breathe and pull away,
the room exhales.

What leaves with the smoke
does not return.

I breathe,
and name the space mine again.

8. Alone

I walk a path
alone.

You walk beside me
alone.

Through crowds
alone.

At a party
alone.

Just the two of us
alone.

join me?

9. Before It Fades

Winter's blanket
has incubated earth's
nascent inhabitants.

White, cold, thick—
it insulates,
enveloping green leaves
as they push through.

Buds of purple
dot the blanket
before it fades.

10. Interlude I: The Quiet Between

The words have landed.
Their echoes still move
through bone and breath.

Silence waits—
not empty,
just listening.

11. Well-intended white woman

Privilege

whiteness

sorrow

guilt

how do I make up
for eternity?

12. Voyeur

"Join us," you said.
Everyone
will be there.

I stood in the rain,
watching you laugh—
a gentle touch.

Your moon tonight,
or hers?

Rain
pours
down.

You beckon.

But the door
is
locked.

13. Reflection

Smudges web the glass—
maps of where I've searched
for something worth keeping.

Steam from the shower drifts upward,
a veil between judgment and grace.

I trace my face in the blur,
learning the shape of forgiveness,
not perfection.

Light shifts.
I see her—
the woman who stayed.

My mouth softens,
edges curling toward warmth.

Tomorrow,
I'll try to see her sooner.

14. Between Breaths

I see you
across a room,
a city,
a state,
a country.

I reach out—
only air.

Nothingness responds.

My soul shatters
into the dark between breaths.
You fade
into my pillow.

I wake to tears—
what's left to hold

15. Side Effects

Mind melting,
feeling jumbled,
confused and numb.

Pink and blue
little pills
dulling it all.

But what about
wanting it—
jumbled, crazy,
happy, sad,
up, down, sideways,
laughter, tears?

What about
feelings?

16. Island Inpiration

A film of mist clings to my skin.
The cold lodges in my chest,
fog swallowing the world—
the trees, the island,
gone to silence,
a shrouded memory.

Then—white feathers.
Two swans, deliberate and still,
push through the lake's curtain,
gliding on the water,
not on my skin.

The world shifts.
Swords of sunbeams pierce
the gloom,
claiming the day.

The island steps forward
to welcome the travelers.

My heart begins to thaw.
If the island can return,
so can I.

17. The Beach

The churning ocean
pounds
all it can reach.

It manspreads across the sand.

There is no room for me.

18. Rubber Band

I stretch me
every day.

An exhausted
rubber band.

Same me,
different shape.

(quiet)
I will
bounce back.

19. Interlude II: The Turning

Something loosens
in the roots of me.

Not growth yet,
not letting go—
just the first hum
of what's shifting.

20. She Stands

She stands
naked on the hillside,
arms raised to meet the clouds.

A blanket of leaves
scattered at her feet.

She is ready
for winter.

21. Standing Against the Gale

The storm is coming—
the wind has changed.
Raindrops question my choices.

I walk the gravel path.
Branches bend as I pass;
leaves glide past,
offering new directions.

Roots sprawl across,
grabbing at my feet.
I sidestep—
a storm-born dancer.

A chipmunk darts ahead,
slips under a bush,
seeking safety.

I measure my breath,

> each step deliberate,
> standing against the gale.

22. After the Surge

After the surge,
after the rage and roar
of storm,
of sea,
of sky—

comes the calm.

I see it
in your eyes.

23. The Waning: A Symphony of Autumn

The wind beats faster,
waves hurl themselves ashore.
Pebbles collide in applause,
their rhythm uneven, urgent.
The days pull back,
light receding with the tide.

Geese carve the sky into measures,
their notes bright against the thinning light.
Crows respond,
unseen conductors hidden from view.
The trees sway to it—
their leaves clapping bright cymbals of flame.

Crickets scratch a thin refrain,
wings clicking against the chill.
The last bees drift low,
drowsy in the dimming sun.
The forest holds its tongue,

but the hush is music, too—
the pause between movements.

Leaves fall in cascades,
each a note let go too soon.
They spiral, violins unspooling
their final solo across the forest floor.
Even the branches ache with melody,
stretched and humming before silence.

I watch from the margins,
uninvited to the encore.
My footsteps disrupt the tempo;
the wind hesitates,
then folds the sound around me.
I listen until I'm not there at all.

The world exhales.
Color softens.
In the hush between heartbeats,
the next rhythm waits.

24. The Awakening: A Symphony of Spring

Morning opens the curtain,
brighter, earlier each day.
Rain taps the fallen leaves,
a gentle percussion—
a signal to the sleeping buds:
wake.

The river swells,
muscle under melting snow,
pounding its rhythm
against the stones—
spring is coming,
calling the world to rise.

Piccolos of finch and wren
slice through the clear air.
A robin keeps steady time,
cardinals flare their crimson notes.
A blue jay startles the silence—

color turning into sound.

Peepers ring from hidden ponds,
their tremolo stitched with joy.
Dragonflies dart in electric arcs,
their wings whispering glass.
A woodpecker adds his syncopated beat,
a pulse to hold it all together.

Fiddleheads uncurl like green tongues of song,
mushrooms lift their pale percussion.
Moss glistens,
the forest tasting its own thaw.
Color surges reckless and new,
a harmony too young for restraint.

I stand within it,
heart quickening to the tempo—
no conductor, no score,
just another listener
becoming sound again.

The world inhales.
Color brightens.
In the space between heartbeats,
the next crescendo builds.

25. The Pulse: A Symphony of Humanity

Engines growl awake.
Doors slam in rhythm.
Steam exhales from grates,
percussion under cold breath.

Footsteps strike the crosswalk—
syncopated, endless.
Engines complain.
Air brakes stutter.
Someone curses into the wind.

Subway thunder.
Metal grinding metal.
The bassline of existence
shakes the ribs of buildings.

Sirens bend the air,
their pitch sliding—
urgent, alive.

Pigeons scatter,
grey notes muffled in the wind.

Vendors call.
A high-pitched laugh cuts through.
Music leaks from a passing car,
four beats before it's gone.

No melody holds—
just motion,
colliding rhythms,
a pulse too human to contain.

I stand in the middle of it,
heart syncing to the din.
This, too, is music:
our dissonant prayer.

The city inhales.
The lights flare.
Diesel, sweat, and heartbeat—
the song goes on.

26. Absorption

White foam presses close,
a slow, deliberate tide.
Water circles what's left of me,
eroding the solidity of my humanity.

Sand clutches at my feet,
pulling like a forgotten memory.
Footsteps vanish
before they offer a clue
to where I was—
the sea already rewriting me.

I try to move,
but the pull deepens.
Gravity and water collude.
Each breath thickens,
each heartbeat drifts toward still.

Seagulls step nearer,
their shadows crossing mine.

They tilt their heads—
I no longer startle them.
Their cries hollow the air
where my name used to be.

The tide rises higher,
and I do not resist.
I am sediment, salt,
the slow surrender of shape.
Even the horizon forgets
where I end.

27. Suspension

Between tides,
I hover—
skin kissed by salt and sun,
bones held light as driftwood.

The water hums its low refrain,
neither pulling nor freeing.
Each heartbeat a small ripple
against the vast unspoken.

Sound cannot find me here.
Even the gulls fade,
their cries softened
by the sea's slow breathing.

Light wavers in the shallows,
time forgets its pulse.
I surrender to the quiet weight
of being held.

Here,
I am both body and breath,
the still point
learning how to move again.

28. Interlude III: The Light Returns

Stillness stretches thin,
and light begins its slow reach.

I do not move,
but I am moving.

29. Thaw

The sun glances off the lake,
fifteen degrees and climbing.
I step into the light,
my breath a small rebellion
against the cold.

The path remembers me.
Gravel shifts beneath my boots,
ice sighs near the shore.
I call your name to the wind—
it answers in fragments.

The trees bend toward my voice,
listening.
I skip a log out of habit,
pretend you're watching,
pretend it matters.

Deeper in the woods,
the air sharpens.

I press my palm to a trunk,
borrow its steadiness.

Without you,
my heart learns a different rhythm—
quieter, but still mine.

30. The Quilt

There's a quilt
just beyond my window,
stitched from the forest's hand—
memories of days past,
threads of what's to come,
history and possibility.

Dark evergreen, steady and deep,
anchors the pattern,
a constant through all change.

Yellow leaves of hesitancy,
one foot in summer,
one brushing the chill of winter.

Orange transitions, committing to change.
Red, rare and resolute,
burns forward with pride and joy.

I watch this quilt of color shift,

moving fabric through my own machine,
envying nature's effortless design.

31. In the Small Things

My day starts with love

You get up
Just to make me coffee
Pack the kids' lunches
Take the dogs for a walk

My day stays in love

You take chores
Washing the laundry
Making sure I eat
Picking the kids up

My day is submerged in love

Hugs and stories of their day
Wagging tails when I glance their way
Smiles from my glance at you

My day ends in love

A TV show together
Your arm around me
Your lips against mine
I slide into sleep

32. Reality

Love is

cleaning the house at ten at night
cooking dinner after a long work day
filing taxes ion a sunny Saturday
folding the laundry (not even mine)
scrubbing the floors ona quiet Sunday

Love is

quiet loud
beautiful ugly
hard work effortless

Love is
all around me

33. Threshold

The washer hums its tired song.
Dinner waits,
half-made, half-forgotten.

I stand in the doorway,
holding a towel,
the scent of clean and lemon thick in the air.

Outside, dusk presses its face to the glass.
Inside, the house keeps breathing,
steady, unaware.

Then something stills—
a drop of quiet
between the rinse and spin,
the part where I remember
who I was
before the noise.

34. Drip

Drip.
The faucet counts the seconds.

Drip.
A tear answers back.

I leak love —
slow, steady,
a rhythm no one asks for.

It seeps into the grout,
the seams,
the places I've patched too many times.

I tell myself I'll fix it tomorrow.
But tonight,
I listen
to what refuses to stop.

35. Negotiation

just a little more time

snooze
covers
dark warmth

coffee first

then maybe
shower

36. Soaring

Soaring above,
I look down on my life.
Up here, nothing can touch me—
I'm free.

Untethered from the day to day,
life's troubles shrink,
softened by distance.

That bill, that call,
those little demands—
minuscule now.

I glide the steady breeze,
weightless among clouds,
loosed from the noise
of the world below.

And still,
I rise.

37. Sinking

I sit up in bed,
ready to tackle the day.
Both feet on the floor—
they sink.

Beyond the carpet,
the floor, the foundation—
nothing solid under me.

Our relationship
is
sinking.

38. Ascent

I rise,
not fast,
not clean—
just steady.

The weight loosens first at the shoulders,
then the heart,
as if belief itself
has softened its grip.

Air tastes new,
thin with promise,
light meeting me halfway.

I do not look down;
gravity will find me soon enough.

For now,
I lift through silence,
each breath widening into grace,

the world unfolding beneath me—
quiet,
whole,
alive.

39. Multiverse

The multiverse hums—
a thousand versions of me
breathing in sync,
out of step.

Somewhere I am sunlight,
sharpened and sure.
Somewhere I am shadow,
curled around regret.

Worlds fold and unfold—
a shimmer, a breath,
possibilities colliding.

I glimpse them:
the mother,
the warrior,
the dreamer,
the woman who stayed,
the one who ran.

Each self reaches back,
fingers brushing through light.

I feel their pulse in mine—
a chorus of maybe.

Perhaps there is no jump—
only unfolding.

40. Fractals

Infinitely repeating,
each pattern folds inside itself—
measured yet untamed,
a quiet symmetry
holding everything together.

A kaleidoscope of order and accident,
turning without our hand,
each fragment choosing
its own reflection.

I see them everywhere—
in shells, in petals,
in mountains reaching toward cloud.
Their rhythm hums through me,
a steady balm against the noise.

Within my body, too, they move—
breath and blood in spiral flow,
currents threading bone and vein,

the hidden math of being alive.

And when the stars appear,
their light repeats the story.
I watch their mirrored dance,
draw in breath—
and wonder,
what vast design
could ever hold
a pattern such as mine?

41. Epilogue: Reentry

I open the door,
the same one I left through—
but it no longer fits the same light.

The air greets me,
a familiar stranger,
soft with new knowing.

The floor still creaks,
but the sound has changed—
a higher note,
less echo,
more song.

I step inside,
not home again,
but onward—
each breath
a turning upward
in the spiral of becoming.

www.ingramcontent.com/pod-product-compliance
Lightning Source LLC
Chambersburg PA
CBHW060353050426
42449CB00011B/2968